Science at Work in
AUTO RACING

By Richard Hantula

Science and Curriculum
Consultant:
Debra Voege, M.A.,
Science Curriculum
Resource Teacher

Marshall Cavendish
Benchmark
New York

Published by Marshall Cavendish Benchmark
An imprint of Marshall Cavendish Corporation

Website: www.marshallcavendish.us

This publication represents the opinions and views of the author based on the author's personal
experience, knowledge, and research. The information in this book serves as a general guide only.
The author and publisher have used their best efforts in preparing this book and disclaim liability
rising directly and indirectly from the use and application of this book.

Other Marshall Cavendish Offices:
Marshall Cavendish International (Asia) Private Limited, 1 New Industrial Road, Singapore 536196 •
Marshall Cavendish International (Thailand) Co Ltd. 253 Asoke, 12th Flr, Sukhumvit 21 Road,
Klongtoey Nua, Wattana, Bangkok 10110, Thailand • Marshall Cavendish (Malaysia) Sdn Bhd,
Times Subang, Lot 46, Subang Hi-Tech Industrial Park, Batu Tiga, 40000 Shah Alam, Selangor
Darul Ehsan, Malaysia

Marshall Cavendish is a trademark of Times Publishing Limited

All websites were available and accurate when this book was sent to press.

Library of Congress Cataloging-in-Publication Data
    Hantula, Richard.
        Science at work in auto racing / Richard Hantula.
            p. cm. — (Sports science)
        Includes bibliographical references and index.
        Summary: "Explains how the laws of science, especially physics, are at work in auto racing"—
    Provided by publisher.
        ISBN 978-1-60870-586-3 (print) — ISBN 978-1-60870-731-7 (ebook) 1. Automobile
    racing—Juvenile literature. 2. Physics—Juvenile literature. I. Title. II. Series.
GV1029.13.H36 2012
796.72—dc22   2010052781

Developed for Marshall Cavendish Benchmark by RJF Publishing LLC (www.RJFpublishing.com)
Design: Westgraphix LLC/Tammy West
Photo Research: Edward A. Thomas

Cover: Cars speed down a wet track in a Formula 1 race.

Printed in Malaysia (T)
135642

CONTENTS

Words defined in the glossary are in
bold type the first time they appear
in the text.

CHAPTER ONE

Raw Speed

Two Top Fuel dragsters speed toward the finish line at a raceway in California.

Picture a drag race. Two cars stand side by side. They get the start signal, and they take off. Each driver wants to be first across the finish line. This is straight ahead, just a quarter of a mile (400 meters) away.

It's a simple race. The drivers don't worry about things like making a turn or saving fuel. Their only concern is moving really fast. They don't even have time to think about anything else. The fastest **dragsters** hit the finish line in five seconds. It takes them less than a second to reach 100 miles (160 kilometers) per hour. At the finish, they may be going more than 330 miles (530 kilometers) per hour.

Relying on Science

Other kinds of auto races don't feature such fantastic speeds. Most races cover longer distances and are run over more complicated racecourses. Some races take place on real streets and roads. However, no matter where and under what rules a race is held, going fast is always the key to winning.

In order to make a high-performance race car, the designers and builders need to know the science behind how vehicles work and move. Drivers need to use some of this science during a race.

Two branches of science are very important for race cars. One is **chemistry**. It deals with substances and materials and how they interact. High-performance race cars are made of special materials and typically burn special fuels. The fastest dragsters, for example, belong to a class called Top Fuel. These cars use a fuel made up mostly of a substance known as nitromethane.

FERDINAND PORSCHE

Today, most race cars are designed by groups of people. Each person knows a lot about one part of creating the car. One person might deal with just the engine. Another person might deal with the car's shape. This person focuses on how to make the car **aerodynamic**—able to slip smoothly through the air. Ferdinand Porsche did it all.

Porsche was born in 1875 in an area of Europe that is now part of the Czech Republic. As a boy, he loved to do experiments with electricity. His career as a car designer started with electric cars. Then, he turned to designing cars that burn fuel. He came up with ideas for both race cars and cars for everyday use. In the 1930s, he designed the Auto Union P-car (the P stood for "Porsche"). This racer had 16 cylinders. It won half of the 64 races it entered, and it set a number of world records. Also in the 1930s, Porsche helped create the Volkswagen Beetle.

In some races, Porsche himself was behind the wheel. In 1910 (see below) he won the long-distance Prinz-Heinrich Race in an aerodynamic car he had designed. He reached speeds of up to 90 miles (140 kilometers) per hour—very fast for that time.

Porsche died in 1951. In 1999, the Global Automotive Elections Foundation named him Car Engineer of the Century.

Nitromethane fuel can produce much more power than ordinary gasoline. It can be dangerous stuff, however. When it burns, the fumes it produces contain the poisonous gas carbon monoxide along with a strong acid—nitric acid. Race crews and other people working near a Top Fuel dragster often wear gas masks.

Another branch of science is very important for understanding race cars in action. This branch of science is called **physics**. It deals with, among other things, how objects move. It explains things that affect the movement of a race car. Scientists who study physics are called physicists.

First Law of Motion

The movement of a race car—and in fact any object—obeys a few basic rules. The English scientist Isaac Newton described these rules in the 1600s, and they are sometimes called Newton's laws of motion. The first law of motion says that if an object is at rest—that is, not moving—it will stay at rest unless some **force** acts on it. The force could be anything that pushes or pulls the object. The first law also says that a moving object will keep moving at the same speed and in the same direction unless some force acts on it.

This feature of an object—staying at rest or staying in motion unless a force acts—has been given a special name by scientists. They call it **inertia**. Inertia, in other

PHYSICS FACT

First Law of Motion
If an object is at rest, it will stay at rest unless a force acts on it. If an object is moving, it will keep on moving in the same direction and at the same speed unless a force acts on it.

words, is an object's tendency to resist a change in its state of motion.

The first law explains a lot about what happens in a drag race. At the beginning of the race, the dragster is at rest. When the race starts, the engine provides a force that is passed to the wheels, causing them to turn. They push against the ground, making the car move. The engine keeps supplying force, making the vehicle go faster and faster. Once the car crosses the finish line, the engine can stop supplying power. That won't stop the car, however. Its inertia will tend to keep it moving. In real life, however, the car slows down and stops. The second part of the law says that this slowing down must be due to the action of a force.

Forces in Action

Actually, several forces act to slow down the dragster. The most obvious one comes from the car's brakes. Brakes use a force called **friction**. This force resists the movement of one object across the surface of another. When the driver applies a car's brakes, the brakes press against a surface in each of the rapidly turning wheels. The resulting friction makes the wheels turn more and more slowly until they stop turning.

Even if the brakes are never applied, the car will not keep coasting forever after the engine is shut off or the driver shifts into neutral gear. Other forces act to slow down the car and stop it. One is a friction force called rolling **resistance**. This is the friction that comes from the contact of the tires with the road.

Another force that slows down the car is caused by the air. Air resists the movement of objects that are traveling

Air Power

It's easy to test the power of air resistance. A passenger in a car going 65 miles (105 kilometers) per hour on the highway can do this. Just stick your hand out the window with the palm facing in the direction that the car is going.

Your hand will feel a powerful force from the air. If you then hold your hand flat, like a wing, you will feel a much smaller force. In this position, your hand is able to move more smoothly in the air. It is more aerodynamic.

through it. This resistance force is called **drag**. For an object moving slowly, this force is weak. At high speeds, drag can be very strong.

Types of Energy

Another idea that physicists use to help explain the movement of objects is **energy**. Energy is the ability to do work. It is the ability to make things happen.

There are different forms of energy. Heat is one form of energy. Electricity is another. Motion is a form of energy called **kinetic energy**. The energy contained in a fuel is known as chemical energy.

Putting Energy to Work

Energy cannot be created or destroyed. It is, as physicists say, always conserved. However, energy can be changed from one form to another. Race cars depend on this fact about energy.

In most race cars, the engine burns fuel. This changes the chemical energy in the fuel into heat. The heat is then used to produce kinetic energy. Electric race cars change electrical energy into kinetic energy.

When a car slows down and stops, its kinetic energy cannot simply disappear. It must change into some other form. One obvious form is heat. When a driver applies the brakes, the car slows down, and the brakes get hot. Some race cars' brakes get so hot they glow.

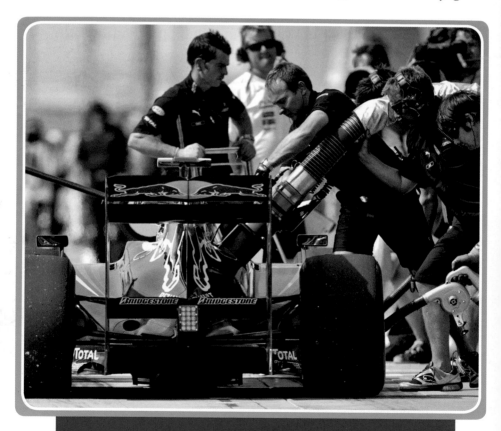

Fuel is put into this race car during a pit stop. Inside the car, the chemical energy in the fuel will be changed first into heat and then into the kinetic energy that makes the car move.

Green and Chocolate

Race car fuels of the future may be very different from the fuels used today. The world's supply of oil, the source of such fossil fuels as gasoline and diesel fuel, is running out. Also, more and more people are concerned about harmful gases released into the air when fossil fuels are burned. The American Le Mans Series of sports car races has helped draw attention to this issue. In 2008 it introduced a Green Challenge competition based on cars' speed, fuel efficiency, and impact on the environment. Better scores go to cars that use less energy and less fossil fuel and that give off smaller amounts of harmful gases.

In 2009, researchers at England's University of Warwick showed an example of what can be done to make cars greener, or friendlier to the environment. They made the first green car to meet the requirements for the international group of races known as Formula 3. The race car, called Lola, needs just 2.5 seconds to reach a speed of 60 miles (100 kilometers) per hour. It can go as fast as 135 miles (217 kilometers) per hour.

The car uses fuel made from chocolate and other materials from plants. Some of its parts are made from carrots, potatoes, flax, and recycled carbon fiber.

Scientists at the University of Warwick show off their chocolate-powered race car.

CHAPTER TWO

At the 500

Cars race around the 2.5-mile oval track
at the Indianapolis 500.

Imagine it's the end of May at the huge Indianapolis Motor Speedway in Indiana. It's time for the famous Indianapolis 500—often called the "Greatest Spectacle in Racing." This is no drag race. The drivers have a lot more to think about than just taking off like a rocket and heading straight for the finish line. Instead of 2 cars, there are 33 on the track. To get to the front of the pack, a driver has to be able to safely pass other cars. What's more, the race lasts not seconds but hours. Instead of a quarter mile, the race is 500 miles (805 kilometers) long. The speedway is shaped like an oval. The track is 2.5 miles (4 kilometers) long. Cars have to go around it 200 times to complete the race. Indy drivers have to do a lot of turning.

Picking Up Speed

Still, drag races and Indy car races are alike in one important way. Once the race begins, the cars need to pick up speed. There's another way to say this: they need **acceleration**.

Some people use the word *acceleration* to just mean "speeding up." But in physics acceleration means any change in the motion of an object. The change may be an increase or decrease in speed. It may be a change in the direction of motion. Or it may be a change in both speed and direction.

In physics, the speed of an object in a given direction is called the object's **velocity**. This makes it possible to describe acceleration in a very easy way: it's simply a change in velocity. A race car at the Indianapolis Motor Speedway does a lot of accelerating. Its changes in velocity involve not only changes in speed but also a lot of changes in direction, both because racers keep trying to pass each other and because of the track's oval shape.

PHYSICS FACT

Second Law of Motion

When a force acts on an object, the greater the force, the greater the acceleration it gives to the object. Also, if the same force is used on objects of different masses, objects with less mass receive more acceleration.

Second Law of Motion

The only way a car's velocity can change is if a force acts on it. This is what Newton's first law says. The English scientist also described a second law of motion, which tells how much acceleration a force can give to a car.

The second law says that the acceleration an object receives depends on two things. One is the size of the force. A bigger force will give a car more acceleration than a smaller force will.

The other thing acceleration depends on is the amount of matter in the object. Scientists call the amount of matter in an object its **mass**. If the same force is applied to two different cars, the car with a smaller mass will receive more acceleration. An easy way to tell which car has less mass is to look at their weights, which are related to their masses. The car with the lighter weight has less mass.

An Indy car is smaller and weighs less than the cars used in NASCAR races, such as the famous Daytona 500. Both Indy cars and NASCAR race cars must obey the second

Weight and Mass

Weight and mass are related, but they are not the same thing. Weight is a measure of the force with which Earth's **gravity** pulls downward on an object. Imagine that a car is taken to the Moon, which has a different gravity from Earth's. The car's mass on the Moon would be the same as it is on Earth, but its weight on the Moon would be different.

14

law of motion. This means that in order to reach any given speed, the engine of a NASCAR racer needs to supply greater force to the wheels than the engine of an Indy car. If the same amount of force acts on both cars, the lighter Indy car responds more quickly.

Turns Take Force

When a car makes a turn, its velocity changes. The driver typically slows down in order to more easily do the turn. But speed is not the only part of velocity that changes. The direction of the car's motion also changes. The car's inertia, however, makes it resist change. The car wants to keep going forward in a straight line. In order to make the turn, force has to be used to overcome this inertia. It is applied through

DANICA PATRICK

Danica Patrick (shown below at the 2010 Indianapolis 500) is the most successful woman Indy car driver ever. She was born in 1982 in Beloit, Wisconsin. Like many other famous racers, she first made a name for herself in the small four-wheeled racing cars called go-karts. In 2005 she drove in the Indy Car Series and was named Rookie of the Year. In that year's Indianapolis 500, Patrick came in fourth, the best finish by a woman in the race's history up to then. Four years later she beat that mark with a third-place finish. In 2008 she became the first woman to win a major Indy car race, the Indy Japan 300. In 2010 Patrick also began racing in some NASCAR events.

Indy vs. Stock

The race cars that take part in the Indianapolis 500 and similar races are known as open-wheel cars. The wheels are located outside the body of the car. There are no guards, or fenders, over the wheels. Also, the driver sits in an open seat. There is no roof covering the driver.

NASCAR cars are called stock cars because they look sort of like ordinary cars. Inside, however, they are very different. NASCAR cars have super-powerful engines and other equipment to improve the car's performance.

An Indy car may weigh about 1,600 pounds (725 kilograms). A NASCAR racer may weigh about twice that much. For this reason, a NASCAR car carries a more powerful engine than an Indy car.

Races in many countries feature open-wheel cars belonging to classes such as Formula 1 and Formula 3. Cars in these classes are even lighter than Indy cars.

NASCAR driver Jimmie Johnson celebrates after winning a race.

the tires, which are pushing against the road. The driver makes the wheels turn, creating a force directed toward the inside of the turn.

The amount of force required will be greater for heavier cars or for cars going really fast. Such cars are said to have

Turning Takes Force

Inertia

Inertia makes this car want to keep going straight.
For the car to turn, force has to be used to overcome
the inertia.

more **momentum**. Momentum is a measure of motion used
in physics. It depends on both the mass and the velocity of
the moving object.

The same factors apply when an ordinary passenger
car turns a corner. Because of inertia, the car wants to keep
going straight. Force is used to make the car turn. The
people sitting in the car also have inertia. Because of their
inertia, their bodies try to keep going straight ahead. The
turning car pushes against the riders, carrying them along
with it into the turn. For the riders, however, it feels as if
some force is pushing them toward the outside of the turn.
This is sometimes called **centrifugal force**. But it is actually
just inertia. There is no real force pushing outward.

CHAPTER THREE

Sticky Force

NASCAR racers speed around one of the banked turns at the Talladega Superspeedway.

Sometimes speed can be a problem. Suppose it's the last lap of a race at the Indianapolis Motor Speedway. The lead car approaches the turn before the final stretch. Another car follows close behind. The cars slow down a bit to make the turn. But the driver of the lead car is too eager to clinch the win and doesn't slow down enough. The car begins to slip as its tires lose their grip on the track. The driver fights to recover control but loses too much speed in doing this. The car running just behind sneaks by, and it manages to reach the finish line first. The lesson is clear: it's very important for tires to keep their grip.

Friction Grip

The key factor in the ability of tires to stick to the road is the friction between the tires and the road surface. There's a limit, however, to the strength of this sticky force, or traction. If a car enters a turn with too much speed, its momentum will overcome the tires' grip. The driver turns the wheels in the direction of the curve. But inertia makes the car try to go straight. The result: the tires slip. In a severe case, the car may skid and crash.

Traction depends both on the road surface and on the car's tires. A surface covered with ice, water, or oil, for example, will be slippery. It is harder for tires to grip a slippery road.

Types of Tires

A tire's ability to stick to the road also depends on its contact patch—the part of the tire in contact with the road. A contact patch with a big area has better traction. That's why many race cars have wide tires. For example, NASCAR cars may be called "stock" vehicles. But they use tires that are wider than the tires on passenger cars.

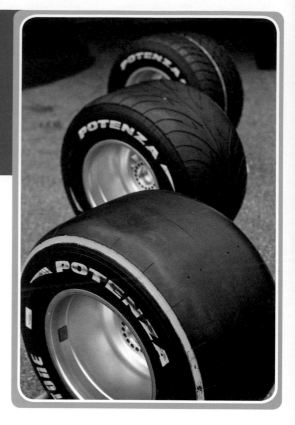

This picture shows three types of racing tires. They are (top to bottom): a tire with a deep tread for very wet weather, a tire with less tread for when the weather is not as bad, and a smooth tire with no tread for racing on a dry track.

Also, in order to make sure that as much tire material touches the ground as possible, cars in some types of races on dry surfaces have smooth tires, with no tread. This improves traction, letting the car go faster. When it rains, however, racers may use tires with a deep tread, which lets water flow away. Tires used on dry tracks are typically softer than ordinary tires. This also improves their grip.

Hot Brakes

Tires are not the only things on a race car that rely on friction to do their job. Friction is equally important for the brakes. They work by pressing against a part of each wheel. The friction between brake and wheel causes the wheel (and the car) to slow down. In the process, the brakes get hot. This is because the car's energy of motion—its kinetic energy—has to go somewhere. (Remember, energy cannot be destroyed.)

Using Waste Energy

When brakes slow a car down, the car loses a lot of kinetic energy. Most cars don't use it for anything. The kinetic energy turns into heat, which is simply allowed to flow away into the air or into nearby parts of the car. The rules of some races, however, allow cars to put this energy to good use. A special system—called a kinetic energy recovery system—stores it in some way. The energy then can later be used to give the engine an extra boost of power. In 2009, Formula 1 racing began allowing kinetic energy recovery systems. The energy can be stored in various forms, such as electrical energy in a battery. The energy can also be stored as the kinetic energy of a rapidly spinning wheel (called a flywheel) inside the car.

When a race car driver applies the brakes, most of the car's kinetic energy changes into heat.

When the driver applies the brakes, the kinetic energy gets turned into heat energy. In addition, some of the energy may turn into light energy. In some racers, such as Formula 1 cars, the hot brakes can glow red or yellow.

Third Law of Motion

Brakes can slow or stop a car because they put to use a third law of motion that was described by Isaac Newton. This law says that when one object exerts a force on another, the second object also exerts a force on the first. The two forces are equal in amount but act in opposite directions. This idea is sometimes said in another way: For every action there is an equal and opposite reaction.

When a driver applies the brakes, the brakes make the tires push against the ground. This force is met by an equal and opposite force from the ground, which pushes against the car. Nothing much happens to the ground when the car pushes against it. The ground is part of Earth. Earth's mass is far too great for it to be affected by the push. The car, however, is much, much smaller. When the ground pushes against it, there is a clear result: the car slows down. The second law of motion explains why this happens: when the same force is applied to two different objects, the object with less mass will receive more acceleration.

PHYSICS FACT

Third Law of Motion

When one object applies a force to a second object, the second also applies an equal force to the first. In other words, for every action there is an equal and opposite reaction.

Banking During Turns

Because there are limits on the ability of tires to grip the road, cars have to slow down when they enter a turn. Some racecourses, however, have banked turns, which don't require as much loss of speed. When a turn is banked, the track's surface slopes inward in the direction of the turn. With a flat turn, the momentum of a speeding racer tends to carry the car off the track. The banking helps cars stay on the track. The tilted surface counteracts some of the car's momentum.

The turns at Talladega Superspeedway in Alabama have especially steep slopes of 33 degrees. At 2.66 miles (4.28 km),

Not an Easy Job

Race car driving requires much more than just getting behind the wheel and heading down the racecourse. Indy car, Formula 1, NASCAR, and other types of races are grueling. Drivers need to be able to focus their minds on a race that may last hours. They also need to be physically fit.

Racing through turns at high speeds puts huge stresses on the body, especially the head and neck. Heat inside the car can be extreme. Drivers may lose several pounds of weight from sweating. Some experts compare driving a Formula 1 race to running a marathon.

Talladega is the longest oval track used by NASCAR. Thanks to the track's long straightaways and steep banking, some of the highest speeds in NASCAR history have been recorded at Talladega.

In the interest of safety, NASCAR in 1988 tried to limit how fast cars could go. It began requiring cars at Talladega (and Daytona, which also has banked curves) to use a device called a restrictor plate that limits engine power.

Race cars moving at high speed can be hard to control. Shown here: Indy driver Mario Moraes gets out of his car after a crash.

CHAPTER FOUR

Air Force

Ryan Newman (left) crosses the finish line to win the 2008 Daytona 500.

Ahole in the air helped Ryan Newman win the Daytona 500 in 2008. The final lap began with veteran driver Tony Stewart in the lead. Newman and several others followed close behind. Stewart stayed in front of Newman, blocking him. But Stewart then moved to an inside lane. Meanwhile, Kurt Busch, a teammate of Newman's at Penske Racing, came up right behind Newman. The two cars were in single file. They formed a **draft**—a sort of hole through the air—that allowed both to go a little faster. They passed Stewart and finished first and second. Stewart ended up in third place.

Drafting

The draft helped Newman and Busch slightly reduce one of the biggest forces acting on their cars: air resistance. Air resists things that try to push through it at high speeds. One form of this air drag occurs because a speeding object presses together the air right in front of it. As a result, the air pressure in this area becomes greater. Air pressure is a force that the air applies to anything in it. At Earth's surface, the air pressure is normally about 14.7 pounds per square inch (about 1 kilogram per square centimeter). People don't notice this force because they are used to it, but it is there. The higher pressure right in front of a speeding car opposes the car's movement. This causes the car's speed to be a bit less than it would be if there were no air.

It's a different story right behind the speeding car. There the pressure is lower than normal. If another car slips into this area, it will find less air resistance than normal. As a result, it can go a little faster than it normally would for the amount of power it is using.

Helmet Safety

High heat, crashes, fire: these are some of the risks drivers face in auto racing. To protect drivers, cars include special safety features, and drivers usually wear special fire-resistant suits and gloves. They also wear helmets. Modern helmets for drivers in high-speed open-wheel races take **aerodynamics** into account. Air flows over the top of a race car at speeds of up to 200 miles (320 kilometers) per hour or more. Aerodynamic helmet design can aid the airflow, keep the helmet from lifting up, and reduce the force of the moving air on the driver's head and neck.

The car in front also benefits. Fast racing cars are designed to be aerodynamic—air flows rather smoothly around them. Still, some disturbances, or turbulence, in the air stream cannot be avoided. This turbulence adds to the drag on the car. One particularly big area of turbulence occurs at the car's rear, where the streams of air rushing around all sides of the car come together. If another car follows very close behind, however, this drag on the first car is reduced. It's as if the two cars combine to form one long car. Or as if they created a hole through the air resistance.

Two or more cars may go in single file this way. This practice is called drafting or slipstreaming. Drivers have to be careful when doing it in a race. The cars are so close together that one wrong move can lead to a crash. But drafting can be useful. It can be used to let all cars in a draft go slightly faster than normal. It can also be used to save on fuel, since slightly less power is needed in order to reach a given speed.

Drafting came in handy for Newman and Busch. They were already getting as much power from their engines as they could. They needed a little extra burst of speed,

Airflow in a Draft

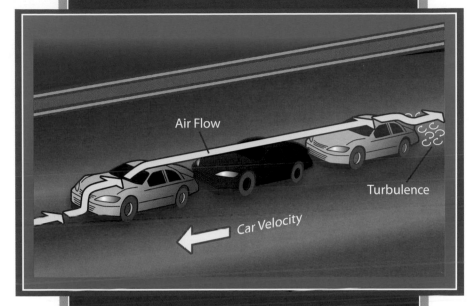

Air Flow

Turbulence

Car Velocity

Air flows more smoothly around cars in a draft. It offers less resistance to their motion.

and they got it from drafting. NASCAR drivers most often use drafting at tracks like Daytona and Talladega, where restrictor plates limit engine power. The restrictor plates and car construction rules generally limit speeds to less than 190 miles (305 kilometers) per hour. Drafting may provide a few extra miles per hour—enough to win the race.

Downforce

Airflow also helps racing cars stick to the ground. This is especially important in fast turns, where the tires' grip on the road may not be strong enough. Race cars are designed so that the airflow produces a force that pushes down on them. This force is called a **downforce**.

Downforce is the reverse of the lift force that makes it possible for airplanes to fly. Airplane wings are designed so that air flowing over and under them produces two different areas of pressure. The air above the wing has a lower pressure. The air below the wing has a higher pressure. The result of this pressure difference is an upward force—lift.

Cars that are moving at very high speeds also may produce lift. Race cars are generally designed to counter this, however. The air above the car should have a higher pressure, and the air underneath it a lower pressure. This pressure difference produces a downforce that helps hold the car on the road.

Air Control

Various devices are used on race cars to improve airflow in order to alter drag or increase downforce. These devices include spoilers, air dams, and wings. A spoiler attached to the rear of the car "spoils" the airflow to reduce lifting tendencies and help produce downforce. The spoiler is often flat—sometimes like a blade—in shape.

An air dam, a sort of spoiler under the front grill, helps keep air from going under the car. This reduces turbulence and airflow beneath the car, improving downforce.

Car wings are the reverse of plane wings. Because of their shape, they produce downforce. They can also help steady the vehicle. Cars may have a wing at the rear or in front, or both. In some cars the driver can slightly change the position of the wing while racing. Some wings have adjustable parts such as flaps.

Side skirts are sometimes used to increase downforce. They redirect air near the ground, so that it passes around

Controlling Airflow

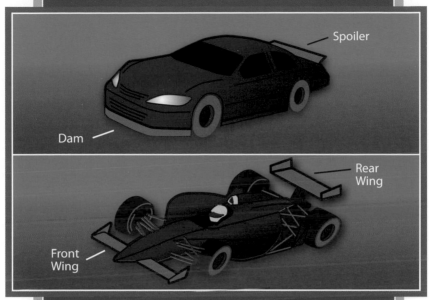

Spoiler

Dam

Rear Wing

Front Wing

Devices such as dams, spoilers, and wings change the airflow around a car. They may produce an increase in downforce or a change in drag.

the car. Side skirts are not allowed in many races, however, because a dangerous loss of downforce can result if a side skirt happens to get knocked off.

Sometimes the bottom of the car is designed to have a special shape, to help increase downforce and reduce drag. For example, air may be directed through tunnels at the bottom of the car.

In planning a car, designers need to take into account the kind of races the car will run. Certain devices may be forbidden by race rules. Designers must also consider whether a device's advantages outweigh its drawbacks. Wings, for example, can increase downforce, but they may also add to drag.

GLOSSARY

acceleration: A change in velocity. As a measurement, it is the rate at which velocity changes.

aerodynamic: Able to slip easily through the air with relatively little drag, the way a race car can.

aerodynamics: The study of the forces that affect an object such as a car or a plane that moves rapidly through the air.

centrifugal force: An outward push that may be felt when making a turn. It is actually an effect of inertia and not a real force.

chemistry: The branch of science dealing with substances.

downforce: A downward force that helps a moving car stick to the ground. It is caused by the air flowing around the car.

draft: Two or more cars going at high speeds very close together in single file. This formation slightly reduces the effects of air resistance on the cars. The use of this technique is called drafting or slipstreaming.

drag: Air resistance; a force that slows an object moving through the air.

dragster: A person or car taking part in a drag race.

energy: In physics, the ability to do work.

force: Anything that causes a change in the velocity of an object, such as a push or a pull.

friction: A force resisting the movement of an object across a surface.

gravity: A force that pulls objects toward the center of Earth.

inertia: The tendency of an object to resist being accelerated. A force has to be applied in order to put into motion an object that is at rest or to change the velocity of an object that is moving.

kinetic energy: The energy of a moving object.

mass: The amount of matter in an object.

momentum: A measure of an object's motion. It equals the object's mass multiplied by its velocity.

physics: The branch of science dealing with matter and energy. Scientists who work in physics are called physicists. They study such things as moving objects.

resistance: Opposition to the movement of an object.

velocity: In physics, the speed and direction of a moving object. Some people use the word to mean simply "speed."

FIND OUT MORE

BOOKS

Gigliotti, Jim. *Famous NASCAR Tracks*. St. Catharines, Ontario: Crabtree, 2008.

Kelley, K. C. *Drag Racing*. New York: Marshall Cavendish Benchmark, 2010.

Kelley, K. C. *NASCAR*. New York: Marshall Cavendish Benchmark, 2010.

Schwartz, Heather E. *The Science of a Race Car: Reactions in Action*. Mankato, MN: Capstone Press, 2010.

WEBSITES

www.circletrack.com/techarticles/ctrp_0707_motorsports_science
This webpage from Circle Track magazine's website talks about the many ways racing relies on science. It includes a link to Circle Track's Young Racers' Club, which has stories about teenage racers' experiences.

www.formula1.com/inside_f1
This section of the official site for Formula 1 tells about rules, safety, and driving Formula 1 cars.

www.indycar.com
This is the official site of the Indy car racing series. It provides information about Indy cars, Indy car races, and Indy drivers.

www.nas.nasa.gov/About/Education/Racecar
This NASA-sponsored website takes a close look at race car aerodynamics.

www.nascar.com/kyn
This section of the official site of NASCAR offers a lot of information about NASCAR cars, drivers, and races.

INDEX

About the Author

Richard Hantula has written, edited, and translated books and articles on science and technology for more than three decades. He was the senior U.S. editor for the *Macmillan Encyclopedia of Science*.